A PORTFOLIO OF

Fireplace Ideas

CREATIVE
PUBLISHING
International

MINNETONKA, MINNESOTA

www.creativepub.com

CONTENTS

This energy-efficient gas fireplace has the ambience of a traditional fireplace with the added benefit of heat circulation. Because the unit burns natural gas, there are none of the cleanup or storage hassles you would have with a wood-burning unit.

This unique configuration includes a fireplace as part of the stunning design of this bar. The direct venting capability of this three-sided gas fireplace allows you to explore any number of nontraditional installations.

WHAT MAKES A GREAT FIREPLACE?

People have always had a passion for fire. It comes from our basic human needs for light, warmth and security. Over time, humans learned how to control fire, and fireplaces and stoves became the heart of the home, the center of food preparation and a warm place to gather with friends and family. The way you plan to use your fireplace or stove will determine which type you choose. If heat is the primary function, you'll want an efficient, heat-circulating model. If your fireplace or stove will have more of a decorative function, you may want to consider a less expensive alcohol-burning unit. Your space constraints, the layout of your room and interior design style will also play a part in your decision.

Today, fireplaces and stoves are not only sources of heat, they are also a way to express an individual style. A fireplace or stove can dictate an interior style, complete a look or add an element of interest to an otherwise ordinary interior. They range in price from a moderately priced prebuilt unit, to a costly conventional fireplace that is built on site. Although many fireplaces and stoves are indeed an investment in the value of a home, their true value comes from the great enjoyment and comfort they add to your lifestyle.

Modern fireplaces and stoves include a number of exciting new technological improvements that make enjoying a fire easier and more satisfying than ever before. Innovations in fireplace and stove designs have produced models that don't have the strict requirements regarding location and clearance. This means that you are no longer limited to the living room or den to enjoy the warmth of a fire. New technology allows us to put a fireplace or stove just about anywhere we wish: in a bedroom, a basement or even a bathroom. There are models to fit almost any space and match any decor.

There are fireplaces and stoves on the market today that burn longer and cleaner than ever before. Many of these newer models use fuel alternatives other than wood. These alternative fuels not only eliminate the hassle of gathering and storing wood; depending on where you live, they can also be less expensive to use. Some types, such as direct-vent gas-fueled models, operate virtually smoke-free and more efficiently than conventional fireplaces and stoves. There are units that burn wood pellets, coal or alcohol, and others that are simply electric heaters designed to look like a fireplace.

FINDING THE RIGHT FIREPLACE

When selecting the fireplace or stove that's best for you and your family, you need to determine what functions your fireplace or stove will need to serve. Consider how often you'll build a fire, and who will be sharing the fire with you. Will your fireplace or stove function as a viable source of heat, as well as an aesthetic element, or will it be strictly a romantic accessory to add atmosphere?

A fireplace or stove needs to be fitted not only to the structural parameters of a space but to the needs of the people using the space. For example, if a home has only one fireplace, it is usually best to locate it where household members gather to relax, converse and entertain, such as in the living room or family room. If a fireplace or stove will be used to warm guests as well as the whole family, the hearth opening needs to be large enough to warm everyone, and the room big enough to hold the fireplace.

Today, fireplaces and stoves can be located in almost any room in the house. The type and style you choose depends on many contributing factors. Interior design style, budget and structural space constraints will rule out some types and styles, but there are many fireplace and stove options that work well in almost any situation.

Fireplaces add warmth, intimacy and beauty to bedrooms, kitchens, dens and bathrooms. Adding the right fireplace can not only warm a room with its heat, it can lend a comforting ambience simply in the way it makes a room look and feel.

This stylish freestanding gas stove *is as efficient with space as it is with heat. The contemporary design takes up minimal floor space and uses natural gas. The large bay door allows users to enjoy the ambience of a roaring fire without the hassles of a traditional fireplace.*

(left) **The focal point of this southwestern kitchen** is an adobe-style wood-burning fireplace. A modern prebuilt metal firebox at the heart of the rustic exterior makes the unit energy efficient. The heat-conducting properties of the cement plaster surround means that the unit will contribute radiant heat as well.

(below) **This space-dividing gas fireplace** lets you view the fire from either side, so one fire can serve two rooms. The direct-vent technology of this unit eliminates the need for a chimney, allowing the surround to have a clean, contemporary look that complements both rooms.

FINDING THE RIGHT FIREPLACE

Both the size and shape of a room play important roles in deciding what size fireplace or stove to buy, and where to put it. But effective and functional placement means more than just correct size and general location. You need to also make sure the location you've chosen allows you to use your fireplace or stove for the reason you intended. For example, putting a fireplace or stove in a room that has an outside door can cause drafts to draw smoke back into the room. Putting some type of barrier between the door and the fireplace or stove will minimize some of these problems. It's also important to locate a fireplace or stove so that people aren't walking in front of a fire while others are warming by it.

Also consider the way a fireplace or stove will affect your indoor air quality. Since fireplaces draw in air as they burn, this can produce drafts or deplete the amount of clean air available for you to use. This is particularly true if your house is very energy-efficient and tightly sealed to prevent incoming cool air from affecting the heated air.

The solution is to consider a direct-venting fireplace or stove. These units are connected directly to the outside by vents which provide all the air needed without drawing it from the interior of the house. Consult your local building codes and contractors to ensure the proper ventilation for the type of fireplace or stove you choose.

Fireplaces and stoves can be divided into two basic categories—those that are built on site and prebuilt units that are made at a manufacturing plant and installed as a unit at the site. Prebuilt units range from a simple fireplace insert that can be placed into an existing fireplace opening, to all-inclusive fireplace and stove units that you simply support, frame and vent. The fuels used in these new fireplaces and stoves include wood, wood pellets, coal, alcohol and natural gas.

Prebuilt fireplaces and stoves come as complete packages that include flues, flashings, caps, etc. The actual work comes with the installation and the cosmetic treatment of the surfaces surrounding the unit. Freestanding prebuilt units need only to be set up and vented; the exterior surfaces are already finished.

Upper Level

Lower Level

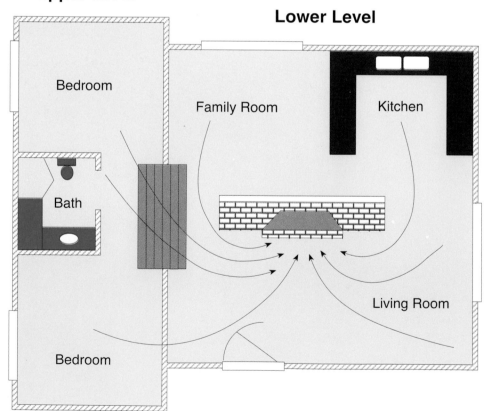

The location of an open-hearth fireplace relative to doors and windows will affect the way warm and cool air move through a house. This floor plan shows how a conventional open-hearth fireplace will suck air from all areas inside the house, sometimes enough to cause interior drafts. If an open-hearth fireplace is located near an exterior door, there could be problems with smoke blowing into the room when the door is opened, as well as problems with cooler air being drawn into the house. Locating a fireplace near a stairwell allows the warmer air to rise to the floor above, distributing the heat more evenly throughout the house.

The convenience of modern, heat-efficient technology combines with the rustic look of an old-fashioned wood stove to create this fashionable and functional wood-burning heat source.

Recent breakthroughs in fireplace design have produced a factory-built insert to fit an arched opening. Until now an arched opening was only available in a conventional masonry fireplace.

(right) **An attractive** Euro-style wood-burning cookstove offers kitchen-friendly features, such as a full-service bake oven that uses radiant heat, and radiant warmth from the unit itself, that make it the center of a cozy, comfortable kitchen.

FIREPLACE BASICS

Fireplaces and stoves produce two types of heat—radiant and convective. Radiant heat is the transfer of heat to various solid objects in a room. Radiant-heat fireplaces don't heat the air space between objects, just the objects themselves. Fireplaces made with heat-conducting materials, such as brick, ceramic, soapstone or adobe, produce radiant heat. They add additional heat to a room by storing the heat produced by a fire and slowly releasing it into the room as radiant heat.

Conventional open-hearth fireplaces, without air vents, are radiant fireplaces. Open-hearth radiant fireplaces alone are inefficient as heat producers. The heat they give off comes mainly from the firebox opening (the place where the fire is built) and only about 10% goes into the room—the other 90% goes up the chimney. Radiant stoves, on the other hand, can be very effective heaters. They are able to produce a substantial amount of heat, which is conducted through the metal walls of the stove.

Convective heat is created by heating the air and circulating it around the room. Convective fireplaces and stoves have two or three walls (depending on the model) around the firebox. Cool air is drawn into these spaces by vents around the fireplace or stove opening and heated as it circulates around the firebox. The warm air is then circulated back into the room, usually through vents above the firebox. Convective fireplaces and stoves are often referred to as heat-circulating. They produce the same amount of heat as radiant models, but by circulating the warmed air they use the heat more efficiently. Some convective units have fans or blowers to circulate the warm air more effectively.

The demand for more heat-efficient fireplaces has resulted in designs that are more efficient than most existing fireplaces or stoves. There are also ways to convert a conventional fireplace to a more efficient unit. For example, a conventional

*A **prebuilt fireplace insert** makes this wood-burning fireplace more heat-efficient and functional. The attractive black metal is a nice contrast to the faux marble finish of the facing.*

open-hearth fireplace can be refitted with a prebuilt, heat-circulating insert with glass doors, and still maintain the look of the original fireplace.

Fireplace inserts are basically stoves that are designed to be placed into the opening of an existing fireplace. They're popular options that can convert a conventional open-hearth fireplace with moderate heating efficiencies into one that is hard-working and very efficient. These units produce both radiant and convective heat, and because they utilize an existing chimney, they eliminate the need to build a new one.

Zero-clearance fireplaces have a double wall around the firebox that cool air circulates through to keep the outer surface from heating up. This allows you to install a fireplace or stove just about anywhere, and opens up an unlimited number of possibilities when choosing what kind of fireplace or stove is right for you.

A radiant-heat soapstone fireplace features a textured midsection with a contrasting dark green surround. Because soapstone retains 2.5 times more heat than brick, a small amount of wood can produce hours of heat.

Anatomy of a Chimney

Cap: *The cap keeps foreign objects from going down the chimney.*

Chimney & flue: *A chimney is lined with a flue, which is made of insulated stainless steel. In some cases a chimney and flue are the same thing. As smoke from a fire rises, it is vented up a chimney through a flue.*

Mantel: *A shelf above the firebox opening that is used for decorative purposes.*

Throat: *The throat is an opening above the firebox where flame, smoke and gases pass into the smoke chamber just below the flue.*

Smoke shelf: *The smoke shelf keeps down drafts from getting down the chimney and blowing smoke back into the room.*

Damper: *The damper is a steel door that opens or closes the throat. It is used to regulate drafts and to prevent heat loss up the chimney, when the fireplace is not in use.*

Firebox: *The firebox can be made of steel or firebrick, a specially made heat-resistant brick; it is the place where the fire is built. The walls and back of the firebox are generally angled in to radiate heat back into the room.*

Hearth: *The inner hearth is made of firebrick or steel, and holds the burning fuel. The outer hearth protects the floor from heat and sparks.*

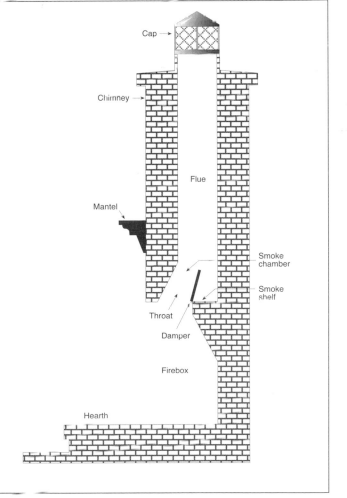

11

FIREPLACE BASICS

Besides the dramatic impact a fireplace or stove will have on an interior room, it will also affect the look of the exterior of your house. If you are installing a conventional masonry fireplace, you will be building a chimney. Be sure to consider the aesthetic impact, such as color and texture, of the materials you use. This material will impact the appearance of your fireplace both inside and outside the house.

Most stoves and freestanding fireplaces have metal chimneys that vent out small pipes through the roof or wall of the house. If your fireplace or stove is not a masonry type, there may be a portion of it, such as a flue, that is exposed on the outside of your house. Most building codes require that any exposed components be enclosed within a chase. A chase is a small room or closetlike structure, without windows or doors, that completely houses the firebox and the flue to both protect and make them more attractive.

There are ways you can use the chase to make an architectural design statement. It can be shaped like a traditional chimney and covered with masonry veneer to resemble an actual masonry chimney. Or if you want to make the chase less conspicuous and less costly, you can build a rectangular-shaped chase and finish it with siding that matches the exterior of the house.

*The **combination of materials** used on this chimney add a dramatic flair to the exterior styling of the home.*

(left) **The rich colors and textures** of the natural stone used to finish the exterior of this chimney are the perfect complement for the woodland setting of this home.

(below) **A combination of cedar siding and natural stone** makes a dramatic statement when used to cover the chase on the exterior of this home.

TYPES OF FIREPLACES

When we imagine a traditional fireplace, most of us picture an open-hearth brick fireplace. The typical brick fireplace is considered a masonry fireplace. And, although the majority of masonry fireplaces are made of brick, other masonry materials, such as natural stone or concrete, are also used. Masonry fireplaces come in both radiant and convective designs. These fireplaces are very difficult and expensive to build, yet they are extremely durable and add their own special ambience to a setting.

A conventional masonry fireplace needs to sit on a reinforced concrete foundation. The walls are generally made of concrete and the chimney is usually made of brick, or some other type of masonry material. Because of their substantial weight, masonry fireplaces must be supported properly, which may create complications when deciding where it should be located. The easiest place to put a masonry fireplace is on an exterior wall, or on a ground level.

Prebuilt fireplaces and stoves come in an array of sizes, shapes and designs, from a basic metal insert to a high-efficiency, "zero-clearance," heat-circulating unit. Prebuilt zero-clearance fireplaces and stoves are a recent innovation in fireplace design. Zero clearance means that these units require minimal clearance from flammable surfaces like walls. They are designed so that cool air circulates between the firebox and the outer surfaces, cooling these surfaces to an acceptable temperature. Because the outer surfaces stay cool enough to safely touch, zero-clearance fireplaces and stoves can be safely installed in almost any space you desire.

Photo courtesy of Vermont Castings, Inc.

Photo courtesy of Austroflamm Industries

A traditional setting for a modern gas insert *captures the ambience of an old-fashioned fireplace, with a lot less work than a wood-burner.*

Prebuilt fireplaces come in a variety of finishes, colors and styles that can add visual drama as well as welcome warmth for a fraction of the cost of a masonry fireplace.

And, if you enjoy the warmth and ambience of a flickering flame but don't want the hassles of a wood-burning unit, there are a number of alternative fuel-burning models to choose from. There are efficient, heat-circulating models that burn natural gas or pellets made from wood by-products, and there are models that are purely decorative, such as alcohol-burning models that produce the effect of a flame but have no real heat-producing properties. Another alternative is a decorative faux fireplace unit that is really an electric heater designed to look like a fireplace.

Photo courtesy of Malm Fireplaces, Inc.

Freedom and flexibility *are the benefits of this freestanding, gas-fueled fireplace. The colorful porcelain-coated steel shell comes in a variety of colors that coordinate with almost any setting.*

A prefabricated fireplace surround *produces the look of a traditional fireplace, even when your fireplace is a not-so-traditional gas-burning model*

15

MASONRY

A conventional masonry fireplace is an open-hearth radiant unit that is built on site. Masonry fireplaces and stoves are usually made of brick, but other masonry materials, such as natural stone, cement or ceramic are also used. An open-hearth brick fireplace is one of the least heat-efficient types of fireplaces. Heating efficiencies can be improved somewhat by adding glass or ceramic doors to the front of the fireplace or stove. A greater improvement can be achieved by converting a conventional open-hearth radiant unit to a convective heat-circulating type.

There are prebuilt fireplace inserts that are essentially wood-burning stoves designed to be placed into existing fireplace openings. These inserts are much more heat efficient because they produce both radiant and convective heat.

Another benefit of these inserts is that they utilize the existing chimney and eliminate the need to build a new one.

Masonry heaters are a close relation to a masonry fireplace and are some of the best producers of radiant heat available. They are different from a fireplace in that they burn a small amount of fuel in the firebox at the beginning of the day, and the heat produced from that fire is then stored within a maze of heat-storing compartments inside the unit itself. The unit then evenly radiates heat into the room for the next twelve to eighteen hours. Because they are made of masonry material, such as brick or soapstone, masonry heaters can look similar to traditional brick fireplaces. They are quite heavy and have the same structural support requirements a masonry fireplace has, but they are much more heat efficient.

Photo courtesy of Lindal Cedar Homes, Inc., Seattle, Washington

Photo courtesy of Masonry Heater Association of North America

***This large masonry fireplace** captures the traditional feel and look of a rustic cabin or hunting lodge. A prebuilt, zero-clearance insert allows builders to keep the warmth and beauty of a conventional masonry fireplace while offering a more efficient source of heat.*

Photo courtesy of Masonry Heater Association of North America

The beauty of a conventional brick fireplace *has been re-created in this extremely efficient masonry heater. Masonry heaters are an extremely efficient source of heat, and there is an unlimited range of masonry facings so you can express your personal style.*

(right) **This massive stone fireplace** *has a distinct three-sided design that produces radiant heat and a view of the fire from all sides.*

Photo courtesy of Heat-N-Glo Fireplace Products, Inc.

A uniquely shaped masonry heater *has all the aesthetic charm of a conventional fireplace. This highly efficient masonry heater keeps this room warm and toasty for twice as long as a conventional fireplace and uses a lot less fuel.*

PREBUILT

Prebuilt fireplaces and stoves refers to units that are factory-built prior to installation. Almost all stoves are prebuilt, and the number of prebuilt fireplaces is increasing every day. Today prebuilt fireplaces and stoves offer an enormous range of possibilities in style and design, as well as location and placement. There are radiant and convective models for almost any type of fuel available, from wood to natural gas.

The many options available in prebuilt fireplaces and stoves offer the flexibility to create almost any fireside setting you desire. Zero-clearance units allow you to create unique and elaborate designs, like those that incorporate fireplaces into tables and bars. If space is restricted, there are compact and unassuming freestanding fireplaces and stoves that can be incorporated into any setting. Although prices vary, prebuilt fireplaces and stoves all share the same basic advantages—relatively low cost, easy installation and flexibility in placement.

Fireplace inserts are another prebuilt option. These prebuilt inserts are basically wood-burning stoves that have been designed to fit into an open-hearth fireplace and vent through the existing chimney. The result is a fireplace that has the look and charm of a high-priced masonry unit, with the heating efficiencies of a modern heat-circulating type.

Prebuilt fireplaces and stoves give you the freedom to create an original fireplace design that adds visual drama and welcoming warmth for a fraction of the cost of a masonry fireplace.

Photo courtesy of Lindal Cedar Homes, Inc., Seattle, Washington

The charm of an old-fashioned open-hearth fireplace *is captured in the beauty of the natural stone facing. The fireplace was made more efficient by filling the opening of the original with a prebuilt heat-circulating insert.*

(left) *A m_____*
prebuilt _____
nicely into the _____
in this massive fireplace
without compromising
the rustic appeal. The
entire wall was faced
with a local stone,
creating a pleasing
complement against the
backdrop of white
drywall and cedar
detailing.

(below) **Prefabricated
fireplace surrounds**
and prebuilt fireplaces
make it easy to find a
unit that will meet your
budget as well as your
needs for heat efficiency
with aesthetic impact.

An old-style stove is tucked into an inconspicuous
corner of the kitchen. Most stoves are easy to install
and are an excellent choice for homes where space is a
limited resource.

19

FREESTANDING

Freestanding fireplaces and stoves can be masonry types, built on site, but most are prebuilt and ready for immediate installation. Many of these freestanding units are made by the same manufacturers of other types of prebuilt fireplaces. The benefits of zero-clearance tolerances and alternative fuel options can be combined to create freestanding fireplaces and stoves that are small, simple room heaters or elaborate, elegant works of art, with fire visible from all sides.

Freestanding wood-burning fireplaces are usually made from either of two different materials; metal or ceramic. The most common is steel. Freestanding steel fireplaces are often cone-shaped, with the bottom, or hearth, raised off the ground. Another type of freestanding wood-burning fireplace is made from ceramic. These units are usually onion-shaped. The materials used in these ceramic units are similar to materials used for the interior of pottery kilns.

Freestanding alternative-fuel fireplaces and stoves offer much more freedom of choice in surface materials, design and style. There are small, European-style units, as well as old-fashioned, antique-looking stoves.

The exterior of a ceramic freestanding fireplace can have a textured glazed surface or a glazed ceramic mosaic tile surface. Both are available in a range of colors. Although the exterior surfaces of ceramic fireplaces are usually safe to touch, they should be placed on a fireproof surface.

Photo courtesy of Austroflamm Industries

This attractive freestanding gas fireplace *is also a heat-circulating unit. The vents above and below the fire opening help circulate warm air throughout the room.*

This unique, coffee table fireplace is an example of a freestanding design that is decorative, as well as an efficient radiant-heat producer. The combustion chamber where the fire burns is sealed and the unit exchanges air for combustion through vents to the outside so the indoor air quality is not affected.

Smart and sleek, this freestanding gas fueled fireplace has a thermostatically controlled blower that circulates warm air around the room.

Beautiful, simple and efficient, this freestanding pellet-burning stove combines the timeless grace of a traditional wood-burning stove with a more efficient and cleaner-burning fuel.

ALTERNATIVE FUEL

In response to the demand for more heat-efficient fireplaces and more flexibility in installation and design, manufacturers have developed a number of fireplaces that burn alternative fuels other than wood.

One of the most popular and versatile types of alternative-fuel fireplaces and stoves uses natural gas. Gas units heat with radiant heat, that comes from the glass and metal surfaces, and convective heat, in the form of warm air currents that circulate around the room. Some units have hand-held remote controls that regulate gas consumption and blower speed for comfort control.

Inserts, fireplaces and stoves can all be found in gas-fueled models. Gas-fueled fireplaces allow more flexibility in finishing, venting and placement options than conventional wood-burning types. Since gas is burned at a much lower temperature than wood, gas units can be placed closer to combustible walls, in many cases without the need of floor or wall protection. Some gas fireplaces require you to construct the surrounding wall, giving you complete freedom to finish the surface any way you choose. Because of the different venting options offered for gas units, such as direct-vent, which requires no chimney, you have more flexibility when determining the placement of a gas unit.

Pellet stoves are the most sophisticated and heat efficient of all wood stoves. They burn small pellets made from wood by-products. They operate much like an old coal burner. The pellets are fed into the fire chamber, where air is blown through to create an extremely hot firebox. The fire burns at such a high temperature that it burns the smoke as well, resulting in a very clean burn and eliminating the need for a chimney. The gases vent through a duct in a fashion similar to a clothes dryer. Pellet stoves are easy to operate, and are much cleaner than wood-burning stoves because the need to cut, haul and stack firewood has been eliminated.

Photo courtesy of La Flame™ Vent-Free Alcohol Fireplaces

This elegant contemporary fireplace *is actually a prefabricated, self-contained surround with an alcohol-fueled fire. The unit offers wood fire realism but is purely decorative.*

Photos courtesy of Austroflamm Industries

Photo courtesy of Heat-N-Glo Fireplace Products, Inc.

Photo courtesy of Rustic Crafts Co., Inc.

Prebuilt fireplaces *allow closer clearances to walls, giving you the freedom to create almost any fireplace configuration you can imagine.*

Clean, cost effective and efficient, a pellet-burning stove uses small wood pellets made of wood by-products—eliminating the chore of chopping and storing wood logs.

Photos courtesy of Theln Co. Inc.

Electric fireplaces are basically decorative electric heaters that have the look of a traditional fireplace. The simulated fire is created using real wood to make the logs, and preformed embers and ashes. Colored electric lights create the effect of a flickering flame.

A pellet-burning stove burns clean, safe, easy-to-handle pellets made from wood by-products. This small unit can heat up to 2,000 square feet.

ALTERNATIVE

Another fuel alternative for fireplaces and stoves is alcohol. Alcohol is safe to burn indoors without venting, because it emits harmless carbon dioxide and water vapor. Preformed log sets have all the texture and detail of real wood logs. The log sets break up the alcohol-fueled flames for a look similar to a real wood fire. Although these units produce a small amount of heat, they are primarily used for decorative purposes. And because they are self-contained, they can be easily moved from one spot to another.

Electric fireplaces are an alternative-fuel fireplace option that will have no installation or emissions problems. Electric fireplaces are essentially electric heaters that give off heat but no flame. They simulate the look and sound of a real fire, without any mess to clean later.

Handcrafted real wood log sets add the realism of wood logs, while preformed embers and ashes add to the authenticity. Colored lights and, in some cases, a gentle crackling sound, are used to create a more realistic fireside atmosphere.

In addition to the many indoor fireplace options available, there are also outdoor fireplaces. Outdoor fireplaces extend the use of an outdoor area well into the evening. Some outdoor fireplaces are gas-fueled while others are basically fire pits and outdoor grills, which use either charcoal or propane gas. Outdoor fireplaces can be as complex or as simple as you desire. They range from elaborate brick and masonry fire pits that are built in as an integral part of a deck or patio, to factory-built gas grills with wheels attached so they can be moved from place to place.

An attractive outdoor alternative, this deck-top fire pit uses conventional masonry materials, such as brick, to capture the ambience of a traditional indoor fireplace.

A portable gas grill can also be considered an outdoor fireplace or stove. The freestanding unit is fueled by a tank of propane gas, and the attached wheels make it easy to move.

Photo courtesy of California Redwood Association

Photo courtesy of Sticks & Stones Innovative Decks and Landscape Design

An outdoor fire pit *is the centerpiece of this outdoor setting. The circular shape coordinates with the shape of the bench to create a cozy alcove around this fun and functional fire pit.*

FIREPLACE & STOVE STYLES

A flickering fireplace is one of the most effective ways to aesthetically influence a room. Even if a fireplace isn't functional, the facing, hearth and mantelpiece become natural focal points in a room.

Adding a new fireplace can be very expensive, but today's built-in and freestanding models offer a number of quick and economical alternatives to conventional masonry types. These newer fireplaces also offer a greater range of versatility in style and finishing materials.

Simply changing the facing, hearth or mantel of a fireplace can make a dramatic difference in its aesthetic impact on a room. If you are trying to make a room seem larger and more formal, you could install a grander fireplace. If there is no existing fireplace, a freestanding fireplace or wood-burning stove is an easy-to-install option that adds character to a room.

A fireplace will become a natural focal point in most rooms. You should think of a fireplace as a major piece of furniture whose character should complement the decor and furnishings. Warm a country-style room with a natural wood mantel and antique fireplace accessories. In a traditional setting, try carved wood paneling, or tile or marble facing. Stone set in mirrors or simple brick works well for contemporary settings, or you can add a painted finish. Enhance the impact by surrounding your fireplace with shelves for collectibles.

Photo courtesy of Pinecrest

*A **finely detailed, hand-carved wood mantel** adds a traditional flavor to the setting. The white marble facing and hearth provide a rich and elegant background that highlights the detailed mantel and the ornate screen and andirons.*

The look of a traditional fireplace was preserved when a high-tech insert was used to fill the old firebox. The arched opening, rich marble and warm brass used on the mantel, facing and hearth enhance the elegant ambience of this room.

TRADITIONAL

When we think about a traditional fireplace style, the classic open-hearth design usually comes to mind. The aesthetic style of the earliest fireplaces was very basic, made of plain wood and comprised of two vertical beams on either side of the opening with a larger beam laid perpendicular across both of them, creating a frame. This was the traditional design of almost all early fireplaces. Mantels evolved as a distinctly separate shelf located just above the opening.

Today a traditional fireplace design consists of a firebox opening trimmed with brick, and a facing made of brick up to the height of the mantel. Other finishing materials for a traditional-style fireplace include marble, stone or wood. An old English pine mantel gives a fireplace a traditional look. Old French marble fireplaces, or copies of them, seem to fit in with almost any style of furnishing and are ideal when upgrading a room. Fireplace inserts are an easy way to maintain the traditional ambience of an existing open-hearth fireplace, and give it an energy-efficient update.

Photo courtesy of La Flame™ Vent-Free Alcohol Fireplaces

Photo courtesy of La Flame™ Vent-Free Alcohol Fireplaces

A taste of French tradition *was captured in the design of this handcrafted mantel and facing. This decorative, alcohol-fueled fireplace offers a maintenance-free fuel system that is easy to install.*

The decorative appeal *of this alcohol-fueled fireplace has the traditional styling of early Americana. The surround has a burgundy cherry finish, a facing made of hunter green tile and detailed moldings and carvings.*

Modern, faux fireplaces, like the electric model shown here, can look almost as realistic as the traditional fireplaces they were designed to replace.

TRADITIONAL

(top right) **A hand-carved, wooden mantel** *re-creates the look of a traditional 18th-century fireplace design. Glass doors and heat-circulating vents, in a brass frame, maintain the classic elegance and increase the heating efficiency of this fireplace.*

(bottom left) **The look of a traditional fireplace** *was re-created in the corner cabinet that surrounds this prebuilt fireplace. Ceramic tile on the facing and hearth adds a subtle contrast and enhances the traditional feel of the fireplace.*

(bottom right) **A modern prebuilt fireplace** *is given a traditional twist with a handcrafted oak cabinet surround, and an oak and tile hearth. The oak was finished with a mahogany stain to blend with the rich warmth of this traditional setting.*

Photo courtesy of Pinecrest

Photo courtesy of Vissan Designs Limited

Photo courtesy of Vissan Designs Limited

*A **rustic stone fireplace** contributes to the look and feel of a traditional mountain lodge in this room. This fireplace's massive facing is built around a conventional masonry fireplace.*

CONTEMPORARY

Contemporary fireplace designs are created for modern interiors, but many work in some traditional settings as well—it's a matter of personal taste. It's common to find contemporary fireplace designs without the detailed mantel or extended hearth seen on traditional fireplace designs. Contemporary fireplaces and stove designs usually have a clean, minimalist look, with elements like the mantel, facing and hearth, less prominent and flush with the wall or front of the fireplace.

Freestanding fireplaces and stoves lend themselves to contemporary shapes, sizes and colors. These fireplaces and stoves often act as a strong sculptural feature and a focal point of the room. If you wish to feature another element as the focal point of a room, look for a simple, clean, contemporary fireplace or stove design that blends subtly with the interior design scheme.

*A **creative design concept** turns a direct-vent gas fireplace into a contemporary work of art.*

***Unconventional colors** and subtle shapes and textures are combined to create an ultracontemporary fireplace.*

A polished marble facing and flush design give this gas fireplace a high-style contemporary flair. *The unique configuration of the fireplace within the wall of windows creates a dramatic visual effect.*

CONTEMPORARY

Sleek styling and subtle contrasts in color *contribute to the contemporary design of this fireplace. This decorative, alcohol-fueled fireplace offers wood-fire realism that can be achieved in almost any room.*

Photo courtesy of La Flame™ Vent-Free Alcohol Fireplaces

This decorative oak fireplace *has a textured marble facing. The elegant design is particularly well suited for a contemporary setting. The fireplace itself is actually an electric heating unit designed to look like a real fireplace.*

Photo courtesy of Rustic Crafts Co., Inc.

Photo courtesy of Lindal Cedar Homes, Inc., Seattle, Washington

Polished chrome adds a contemporary flair to this sophisticated fireplace. The reflective chrome helps maintain the combination of glossy surfaces and monochromatic color scheme that gives the setting a seamless, unified look.

CORNER DESIGNS

A fireplace designed to fit in a corner can be used to illuminate and warm a dark, unused area of the room, filling it with the inviting glow of a fire. Fireplaces designed for corners come in many sizes and shapes, and are finished with any number of materials, from stone and concrete to adobe or metal. The facing you choose will depend on the look and feel you wish to bring to the room.

Many of the stylish designs of the new factory-built models fit neatly into small corners. And, because they don't need as much clearance as conventional fireplaces, they take up even less floor space.

Photo courtesy of Rustic Crafts Co., Inc.

Photo courtesy of Malm Fireplaces, Inc.

This small corner fireplace *is actually an electric room heater. The corner design allows you to put it in an out-of-the-way corner so it takes up less floor space. The Santa Fe adobe design of this unit adds to the southwestern flavor of the room.*

Freestanding fireplaces *are an excellent option when you want a fireplace to fit into a tight corner. The steel shell of this model has a refractory brick lining so it requires only minimal clearance from combustible materials. You can enjoy the beauty of the fire through curved ceramic glass doors or a curved grate that attaches to the unit.*

*A **custom-styled surround** was built around this zero-clearance fireplace unit, into the corner. The surround was finished with plaster to give it the realistic texture and color of an adobe-style fireplace, and ceramic tiles were inset into the plaster to enhance the southwestern flavor.*

CORNER DESIGNS

If you want a fireplace but are strapped for space, a corner design is worth looking into. One of the benefits of fireplaces located in corners is that they take up a small amount of floor space. A corner fireplace is ideal in a bedroom, where it doesn't need to be the focal point of the room and where floor space is often a valuable commodity.

If you'd like your fireplace or stove to be the focal point of a room, a corner design may not be the best choice. Located in a corner, these units will not attract as much visual attention. The corner location also makes it difficult for many people to gather around, and makes arranging the furniture a bit more challenging.

Zero-clearance gas fireplaces *open the options for unique yet practical applications. The innovative design of this direct-vent, gas fireplace allows you to place it in any corner or even between rooms.*

This traditional-looking fireplace *is actually a custom-built masonry heater. It was built in a corner, between two adjacent rooms, for the most efficient heat circulation, and divides the space into various rooms and activity areas. A masonry heater will keep all parts of the room warm and comfortable from early in the morning when the fire is first started to late into the evening, hours after the last fuel is added to the fire.*

SPACE DIVIDERS

New direct-vent fireplace models offer two, three and even four-sided views of a fire. These see-through designs let you enjoy the warm glow of a fire from all areas of the room.

Space-dividing fireplaces are often peninsula- or island-shaped and can be used to mark the division between separate activity areas or as part of a solid wall between two rooms. Many new high-tech fireplaces are designed to operate with closed doors and regulated air intake and exhaust. They are similar to fireplace inserts that are installed into walls, with the same high efficiencies and attractive viewing glass.

The versatility of this direct-vent gas fireplace lets you create a unique architectural design, while offering a view of the fire from adjoining rooms.

The distinct peninsula shape of this direct-vent gas fireplace helps to divide the space in this family room into two separate areas. Innovations in technical design make possible a three-sided fireplace that can be viewed from anywhere in the room.

A massive multisided, peninsula-shaped fireplace is the centerpiece of this room. The natural stone surround gives it the look of a rustic mountain lodge.

SPACE DIVIDERS

The clean, classic look of this peninsula-shaped marble surround complements the modern setting. This heat-circulating fireplace subtly divides the room into two separate areas, and still enhances the contemporary style of the room.

This direct-vent gas fireplace fits flush with the wall and is the perfect choice to maintain the clean, contemporary style of the interior. The rich-looking marble facing is carried around the entire divide, creating a stunning backdrop in either room.

HEARTHS & FACINGS

The hearth is the area of a fireplace that a fire is built on. The portion that extends into the room, called the extended hearth, provides protection from sparks and embers that might escape from the fire. This ledge can also be used to sit on, or as a shelf to display decorative items along. Building codes dictate how far beyond the front and to the sides of the opening a hearth must extend.

Hearths are either flush with the floor or raised above it; space often determines which option is better suited to the room. Small rooms need a flush hearth so traffic can flow smoothly. Raised hearths are better suited to large rooms to create more size for the fireplace and help draw attention to it.

Raised hearths can be solid or cantilevered. Cantilevered types can provide storage underneath for wood. Both types of raised hearths provide a surface to display plants or other decorative objects.

The facing is the vertical surface around a fireplace opening. It is often the part of the fireplace that draws the most visual attention. The facing can be as large as the entire fireplace wall. Common materials used for fireplace facings include brick, ceramic tile, stone, concrete, adobe, wood and various metals.

The materials you choose for your facing will dramatically affect the aesthetic impact a fireplace has on a room. Many striking fireplace designs combine two or more different materials in one facing. Brick and wood are two traditional favorites. Marble, wood and polished brass can be combined to create a warm yet elegant facing with classic appeal that will complement any formal setting.

Instead of a mantel and facing, which are parts of conventional fireplaces, hoods are used on freestanding fireplaces. They are usually made of metal, although some are masonry in a metal frame or plaster over a metal frame. One drawback to hoods is that they don't draw smoke very effectively until they have warmed up. Solid metal hoods heat more quickly, so they are less of a problem than other types.

Photo courtesy of Heatilator, Inc.

A large, wide, extended hearth provides warm, comfortable seating for friends and family gathered around the fire.

The large, natural cut stones used in the facing of this fireplace fit the grand scheme of this rustic setting. The hand-cut style of the stones and the massive wood mantel enhance the rough natural style of the room.

ACCESSORIES

Fireplace accessories can be both decorative and functional. Fire-tending tools are usually made of wrought iron and come in a range of styles. A typical fireplace tool set includes a stand, shovel, poker, a small broom and sometime tongs. More elaborate sets include additional tools, like a bellows.

Cranes can be positioned over a fire to hang pots, and grates, made from steel or cast iron, provide the actual support for the logs. Andirons are primarily decorative and are not necessary for the actual functioning of the fireplace. They act like bookends to keep logs from rolling out of the fireplace. The designs for these accessories range from simple to elaborate configurations.

Screens provide protection from sparks and embers that might jump out of the firebox. There are many styles available. Some screens are free-standing, with rigid frames, and are placed in front of the firebox opening. They can be one-piece designs, or manufactured with one large center panel and two smaller side panels that hinge from each side. Some screens operate like draperies and can be pulled to each side of the opening.

Glass doors use heat-resistant glass and come in many styles and configurations. They increase the heating efficiency of a fire by keeping the warm air in and the cool air out.

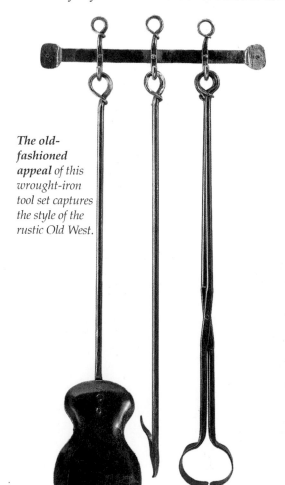

The old-fashioned appeal of this wrought-iron tool set captures the style of the rustic Old West.

Photo courtesy of John Wright Co., Inc.

A colorful stovetop steamer can be set atop a stove for a quick food warm-up, or used to add essential moisture to a room.

Both bottom photos courtesy of Rustic Crafts Co., Inc.

An etched-glass screen turns a fireplace opening into a work of art. The tempered glass has a flat polished edge.

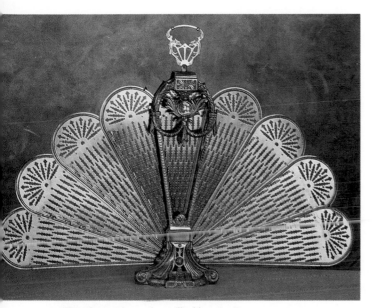

This elegant brass fan will add an Art Deco accent to any fireplace setting. The solid brass fan functions as a fireplace screen.

This polished brass four-fold screen guards against any errant embers and adds an elegant appeal to any fireplace.

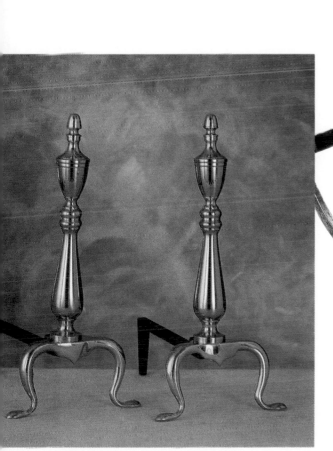

Many accessories add a touch of elegance, like these polished-brass, urn-shaped andirons.

This hand-wrought log basket will last a lifetime. This attractive accessory has a natural iron finish and decorative detailing.

FIREPLACE IDEAS

FAMILY & LIVING ROOM FIREPLACES

A well-placed fireplace or stove can be the perfect addition to a family room or living room. Fire sources foster a feeling of community, and are natural gathering spots for group conversation. If you choose to add a fireplace or stove to your family room, you may find it preferable to a television set.

The fire itself is but one aspect of a family room or living room fireplace. A prominent fireplace mantel can clearly set the tone of the entire room. Best of all, from brick to marble, mantels can be built with materials that match your existing family room decor.

Family rooms and living rooms vary greatly in size. Make sure your fireplace is large enough for the room, but not so large that you bake in your seat. Position the fireplace away from areas of heavy foot traffic or doorways. Obviously, there are many factors to consider, from ceiling height to building codes, so make sure to consult an expert before deciding on a specific fireplace location or style.

A fireplace is often at its best when set against a background of windows. Against a wall of impressive windows, you get two views at once — the roaring fire and the beautiful scenery outdoors. On the other hand, some people prefer the family room fireplace to be tucked away into a discreet corner, adding to the feeling of security and privacy. Either way, a family room fireplace or stove instantly becomes a highlight of the entire home.

Inset photo courtesy of Heatilator, Inc., photo opposite page courtesy of Lindal Cedar Homes, Inc., Seattle, Washington

This huge stone fireplace *actually forms a wall to blend perfectly into this rustic family room decor. Notice the built-in firewood cubbyhole, which provides attractive, clean and convenient storage.*

(right) **This modern, gleaming fireplace blends** *perfectly with the open, angular decor of the room.*

(below) **The stone mantel and simple design** *match the southwestern-style family room.*

Large wood-burning stoves can be the ideal family room heat source. In a large, multilevel room, the heating demands can be great. Rather than incorporating a relatively inefficient conventional open-hearth fireplace, consider a wood-burning stove. Masonry heaters, in particular, are ideal for large family rooms. Modern masonry heaters are often visually impressive and gradually release their stored heat throughout a day.

Made of soapstone, this huge wood-burning, masonry heater is more than a beautiful family room feature—it's an efficient, clean-burning heat source.

Photo courtesy of Tulikivi U.S. Inc.

Conventional fireplaces can still be the best choice. This traditional beauty blends perfectly with the conservative decor of the family room. Glass doors and heat-circulating vents have been added to improve the unit's heating efficiency.

As the main gathering point for a home, the family room should be organized to accommodate the many, as well as the few. Many choose to position their fireplace or stove in a relatively central location in order to spread the enjoyment of it throughout the room.

Photo courtesy of Masonry Heater Association of North America

Positioned ideally *for maximum enjoyment, this custom-designed heat source ensures widespread warmth. The unique design of the surround adds its own aesthetic impact.*

Photo courtesy of Lindal Cedar Homes, Inc., Seattle, Washington

A floor-to-ceiling fireplace, *viewable from both sides, divides this large room into two separate activity areas, and is the centerpiece of both of them.*

(left) **This modern corner unit** *is displayed prominently in the family room as a decorative highlight.*

(below) **Before a fire is even built,** *this traditional brick fireplace brings measurable warmth and ambience to this cool, contemporary interior. Imagine the hours of enjoyment the family must have, gathered around a roaring fire in the comfort of a spacious, well-furnished room.*

59

(left) **This elegant fireplace insert** proves that a stylish alternative to the conventional fireplace can be a beautiful family room feature.

(below) **Stunning yet stylish.** This huge fireplace, finished with large natural stone, provides a wall of soothing warmth and entertainment.

Photo courtesy of Lindal Cedar Homes, Inc., Seattle, Washington

Photo courtesy of Austroflamm Industries

(right) **This family room provides the owners** *with the option of enjoying the scenic view or the extra-wide fireplace.*

(below) **A comfortable sofa,** *in front of the fireplace, and a warm window seat along the hearth, create the kind of cozy setting fireplaces are famous for.*

Photo courtesy of The Majestic Products Company

Photo courtesy of Travis Industries

(left) **The convenience of a fireplace insert** *makes it easy to enjoy a pleasant conversation around a comfortable, clean fire source.*

(below) **The surround of this modern gas fireplace** *is designed to sit flush against the wall—its conservative design is prominent but hardly obtrusive. The brass accessories add the finishing touches for a look of subtle sophistication.*

Photo courtesy of Readybuilt Products

65

DEN & STUDY FIREPLACES

Many people consider a den or study incomplete without a fire source. Sitting at a desk or in a comfortable chair in front of a roaring fire is a classic scene—one of creativity and relaxation. You may be surprised at how much a fireplace or stove can improve a den or study.

Most of these rooms share certain common characteristics that have an impact on fire-source placement. For instance, these rooms usually are enclosed, with one or two entrances. Be aware of the traffic patterns in the room, and position your furniture so that foot traffic doesn't cross in front of the fire. People passing back and forth in front of a fire as they enter and exit a room can be an annoyance, and the drafts created from

opening doors can stir smoke into the den or study. If cleanliness is an issue, you may want to consider putting an alternative fuel-burning unit, such as gas, into an existing fireplace opening. That way, you can enjoy the benefits of a live fire without having to deal with cleanup or hauling wood from outside to the fireplace.

From large, brick fireplaces to small, wood-burning stoves, a fire source can transform your cold, impersonal den or study into a comfortable, thought-provoking haven. With the glowing fire acting as a beacon for your intellectual pursuits, you will find yourself spending more and more time in its friendly, warm confines.

*A **wood-burning insert** fits perfectly into the opening of this large, traditional fireplace and enhances the conservative look of this small study.*

(right) **What's a classic study** *without a roaring fire to cast shadows around the paneled walls? This large fireplace plays the part with style.*

(below) **A soapstone masonry heater** *releases heat throughout the day, even after the wood fuel is spent, to keep any den, no matter how large, warm and comfortable.*

(right) **The traditional elegance** of this marble and wood fireplace was preserved, even when a more economical prebuilt unit was placed in the original open-hearth masonry fireplace.

(below) **A wood-burning stove** is positioned in the hearth, replacing the traditional fireplace with a more efficient design, while maintaining the beautiful fireplace appearance.

Photo courtesy of HearthStone, photo by Stephen Ostrowski

71

(right) **Part bar, part fireplace, all class.** This thoroughly original peninsula gas burner sets the tone for this traditional den.

(below) **Beautiful decorative tile and fine** woodwork surround this wood-burning fireplace insert in elegance and style.

Photo courtesy of Laufen Ceramic Tile

Photo courtesy of Heat-N-Glo Fireplace Products, Inc.

(right) ***A traditional brick fireplace*** *fits smoothly into the decor of this den, which combines the best aspects of a rec room with the treasured privacy of a study.*

(below) ***Polished elegance is the outstanding*** *quality of this den and fireplace, which tastefully displays treasures along the wooden mantel.*

FIREPLACES FOR THE KITCHEN

The kitchen has always been thought of as the heart of the home. A modern kitchen fireplace or stove enhances this traditional idea with practical heat and old-fashioned kitchen ambience. A kitchen fireplace is frequently reminiscent of the days when a live fire was a kitchen necessity, providing cooking heat and warmth for the entire house. Whether a fireplace is fully functional or purely decorative, it will always look at home in the kitchen.

Traditional cookstoves, on the other hand, are still capable of providing vital kitchen functions. In many ways, wood and fossil fuel stoves are preferable to electric stoves. These traditional stoves have been updated with modern features and often provide the dual service of cooking your food and heating your home.

One of the main advantages of traditional kitchen cookstoves is their appearance. Wood or gas cookstoves generally have an attractive, old-style appeal that creates a focal point for the kitchen. Best of all, many of these stoves make cooking and eating a more enjoyable process. Cast-iron models use radiant heat to cook the food—an efficient method that ensures great taste. Some European-style stoves are available to heat the home and cook your food at the same time. These custom-built masonry heaters are generally finished with soapstone, tile, marble or stucco and provide an efficient, attractive kitchen heating source.

It is important to remember that traditional wood or gas cookstoves do not signify an outdated kitchen. Even if your kitchen is thoroughly modern in design, there are plenty of contemporary cookstove options. More and more, these cost-effective heat sources are becoming the stoves of choice for the modern homeowner.

An ornate gas fireplace suits this kitchen and dining area perfectly. With its mantel and accessories it makes the large room warm and comforting.

(left) **A modern gas fireplace** *is the decorative focal point for the entire kitchen. This unusual configuration proves that you can smoothly incorporate an original fireplace into nearly any room decor.*

(below) **This contemporary gas fireplace design** *fits surprisingly well into the traditional Old World style of the surround.*

Photo courtesy of Heatilator, Inc.

(right) **A large, cast-iron stove** combines the look of an antique with the modern advancements of a radiant-heat, gas cookstove. The cast-iron design utilizes radiant heat to cook food. This kind of heat distribution is considered superior to that found in conventional sheet-metal stoves.

(below) **This large kitchen hearth** sets the tone for the entire room. A modern fireplace insert, with heat-circulating vents, increases the heat efficiency, yet maintains the medieval flavor.

Photo courtesy of Travis Industries

A roaring fire provides a glowing accent to this southwestern-style kitchen. Built-in seating allows the homeowners to enjoy the scents of the food and the warmth of the fire simultaneously.

Photo courtesy of Biofire, Inc.

Photo courtesy of AGA Cookers

A small, cast-iron, radiant heat cookstove adds to the rich, warm decor of this traditional midwestern kitchen.

(right) **A loaf of bread bakes** *in the upper compartment of this wood burner, while a fire in the lower compartment warms the kitchen.*

(below) **The soapstone exterior** *of this wood-burning fireplace absorbs the heat of the fire and distributes it gradually throughout the day. This adaptable fireplace includes a generously sized bake oven and two separate fireboxes for flexibility.*

Photo courtesy of Tulikivi U.S. Inc.

Inset photo courtesy of Heatilator, Inc., photo opposite page courtesy of Heat-N-Glo Fireplace Products, Inc.

FIREPLACES FOR THE BED & BATH

Fireplaces and stoves can provide an ideal combination of decoration and warmth throughout a home. Nowhere is this more apparent than in the bedroom or bathroom. Regardless of the fuel type or design style, a bedroom or bathroom fireplace or stove profoundly affects the look and feel of the entire room.

Advancements in fireplace and stove design have expanded the options for the bedroom or the bath. You can position a fireplace as a kind of room divider, or opt for the more traditional corner model. Whether your interest is in the practical aspects of heat distribution, or the aesthetic aspects of your home, these rooms will benefit greatly from an efficient stove or fireplace.

A fireplace doesn't need to be functional to make a decorative statement. Many people choose to keep a well-maintained fireplace mantel and surround in their bedroom or bathroom as a purely visual accent. With the chimney closed off, the fireplace becomes an ideal spot for pottery or flowers. Some prefer only the look of a functional fireplace, and install a type of artificial fire in what was once a working hearth.

In addition to the obvious benefits of heating, the mere presence of a fireplace adds a level of intimacy to the most private areas in your home. Whether you're installing a decorative hearth or a fully functional stove, the look and feel of your bedroom or bathroom can only improve.

This sleek, modern fireplace serves double duty as a room divider and as an impressive centerpiece for the whole room.

(right) **This traditional brick fireplace** functions only as a decorative backdrop for plants and sculpture.

(below) **Positioned in front of a large bank** of windows, this fireplace provides the bedroom with a combination of stunning views.

Photo courtesy of The Majestic Products Company

Photo courtesy of Lindal Cedar Homes, Inc., Seattle, Washington

(right) **A roaring fire**
*is situated in full view
of the bed to provide a
comforting glow
throughout the night.*

Photo courtesy of Heat-N-Glo Fireplace Products, Inc.

Photo courtesy of Rustic Crafts Co., Inc.

(above) **Paintings and statues** *positioned near the fireplace are brought into prominence and share attention with the fireplace itself.*

Positioned between *the bedroom and bathroom, this clever gas fireplace brings intimacy and a romantic ambience to two rooms at once.*

Photo courtesy of Austroflamm Industries

A centrally located *wood-burning stove combines modern efficiency with old-fashioned comfort.*

Photo courtesy of Austroflamm Industries

LIST OF CONTRIBUTORS

We'd like to thank the following companies for providing the photographs used in this book:

AGA Ranges
1-800-633-9200
www.aga.ranges.com

Austroflamm Industries, Inc.
724-695-2430
www.austroflammus.com

Biofire, Inc.
801-486-0266
www.biofireinc.com

California Redwood Association
415-382-0662
www.calredwood.org

Crossville Ceramics
800-221-9093
www.crossville-ceramics.com

FireSpaces, Inc.
503-227-0547
www.firespaces.com

Florida Tile Industries, Inc.
800-FLA-TILE (ext. 4156)
www.floridatile.com

HearthStone/NHC Inc.
802-888-5232
www.hearthstonestoves.com

Heatilator Inc.
A HON INDUSTRIES Company
800-843-2848
www.heatilator.com

Heat-N-Glo Fireplace Products, Inc.
952-985-6001
www.heatnglo.com

John Wright Co. Inc.
800-444-9364
www.jwright.com

La Flame™ Vent-Free
Alcohol & Electric Fireplaces
715-792-2890
www.laflame.com

Laufen Ceramic Tile
800-758-TILE
www.laufenusa.com

Lindal Cedar Homes, Inc.
206-725-0900
www.lindalcedarhomes.com

Malm Fireplaces, Inc.
800-535-7755
www.malmfireplaces.com

Masonry Heater Association
of North America
802-728-5896
www.mha.net

Osburn Manufacturing, Inc.
250-652-4200
www.osburn-mfg.com

Pinecrest
800-443-5357
www.pincrestinc.com

Readybuilt Products
410-233-5833
www.readybuilt.com

Rustic Crafts Co., Inc.
717-969-1777

Superior Fireplace Company
714-521-7302
www.superiorfireplace.com

Sticks and Stones Innovative Decks
and Landscape Design
612-920-2400

Thelin Co. Inc.
800-949-5048
www.thelinco.com

Travis Industries
206-827-9505
www.hearth.com/travis

Tulikivi U.S. Inc.
212-896-3897
www.tulikivi.com

Vermont Castings/Majestic Products
800-227-8683
www.vermontcastings.com
www.majesticproducts.com

Vissan Designs Limited
613-432-8181
www.vissan.com

Waterford Irish Stoves
800-828-5781
www.waterfordstoves.com

President/CEO: Michael Eleftheriou
Vice President/Publisher: Linda Ball
Vice President/Retail Sales & Marketing:
Kevin Haas

Author: Home How-To Institute™
Creative Director: William B. Jones
Associate Creative Director: Tim Himsel
Group Executive Editor: Paul Currie
Managing Editor: Carol Harvatin
Editor: Mark Biscan
Art Director: Gina Seeling
Copy Editor: Janice Cauley
Vice President of Development
    Planning & Production: Jim Bindas
Production Coordinator: Laura Hokkanen

Printed by Quebecor World Dubuque
10 9 8 7 6

Library of Congress
Cataloging-in-Publication Data
Portfolio of fireplace ideas.
p. cm.

ISBN 0-86573-990-0 (softcover)
1. Fireplaces—Design and construction. 2.
Interior decoration.
I. Cy DeCosse Incorporated.
TH7425.P63 1996
721'.8—dc20
96-7947   CIP

Front cover photo and back cover photos
(bottom left and bottom right) courtesy of
Heatilator, Inc.

Back cover photo (top left) and table of
contents photo contributed by Vermont
Castings, Majestic Products.

Back cover photo (top right) contributed
by FireSpaces, Inc., Walter Moberg design.